For Rob
from Bebe
— with a hug !
Advent
2010

D1593497

Lessons In Forgetting

Poems by

Malaika King Albrecht

Author's Choice Chapbook Series

MAIN STREET RAG PUBLISHING COMPANY
CHARLOTTE, NORTH CAROLINA

Acknowledgments:

The author wishes to thank the following editors, journals
and books where these poems first appeared:

Empowerment4Women: "Before They Tell Us What's
    Wrong," formerly titled "Alzheimer's"
Fieralingue: "Cleaning Out Her Closet," "My Father
    Teaching My Eldest Daughter," "My Mother's
    Fever," "My Mother's Transformation," "That
    Wednesday Afternoon," "The Day Mother
    Forgets How to Get Out of the Car," "The Gift"
The Mom Egg: "Mother Leaving the Field of Forget-
    Me-Nots"
Oak Bend Review: "She's Forgotten That She Used to
    Smoke"
13th Warrior Review: "The Growing List"
Wild Goose Review: "The Riddle Song," "One Last
    Time," "The Great Blue Heron Rookery"
Boston Literary Magazine: "Where I Find Her"
Stone's Throw Magazine: "Winging It"

This book is in honor of my parents, Bean and Pop Pop,
with love for my daughters, Amani and Serena, and for Rob,
and gratitude to my many family members,
both of origin and of choice.

CONTENTS

WINGING IT

Years before we knew
of her Alzheimer's,

watching a great blue heron
startle the fog on Menokin Bay,

she struggled to find the bird's
name. She spread her arms and said

Oh, flappity flap jack and laughed,
winging the air. The bird's wings

skimmed so close to the water,
I thought he'd break the surface.

GO FLY A HAT

For Christmas 1950, Mary Catherine got
a kite yellow as a crocus. She flew it
high above Beaverdale Elementary School,
neighborhood kids watching the kite rise
like a gold finch, like the sun, like hope.

My mother ran home, tied her new
Sunday hat to Pop's fishing line,
tossed the hat into air
and sprinted through the fallow corn field
behind her house. The hat bounced

in the snow until a gust flung it into the air.
Her younger brother raced after her,
yelling, *What're you doing?*
My mother kept running and
shouted, *I'm flying my hat.*

Malaika King Albrecht

THE GIFTS SHE GIVES US FOR CHRISTMAS

My 4 year old daughter Amani unwraps
my mom's gift to her
and stares into the box. She says,
Oh, pretty! and tries to stick
Mom's pearl earrings
into her un-pierced lobes.
Later, Sweetie, I say quietly
and tuck the earrings
into familiar kitchen towels
I have just unwrapped.
Open yours next,
she says to my dad.
He tugs the Sunday comics
off the box and gently parts
the tissue paper.
He holds up a purple
suede coat. *Uh, thank you.*
He struggles to slide
his left arm into the sleeve
and reaches behind his back
trying to find the other.
My daughter laughs
watching his right arm flap
while his other arm's caught
tight in the coat.
Mom tugs the coat off him
and slips it on quickly.
Oh, it fits me.
Let me find you
another present.

BEFORE THEY TELL US WHAT'S WRONG

Outside the bay window, pine limbs bend
heavy with ordinary snow. My daughters
tease each other, kick feet beneath
the kitchen table—
        the cherry one you refinished
        for my wedding present—
where my eldest, practicing cursive,
wrote her name into the wood.
        With steel wool you sanded
        every imperfection smooth,
        erased decades of meals.

You sit silent after eating yogurt and Ensure,
your hands folding and unfolding a napkin.
How quietly the afternoon changed
our backyard;
        the curving paths the girls and I
        created to the creek and home
        all summer long, hidden now
        underneath the drift.

Malaika King Albrecht

ONE LAST TIME

Mom and I know this is wrong,
the parking lot, the take-out paper bag
between us, and the car idling,
a/c blasting and her gulping down
Benadryl pills with unsweetened tea.

She reaches into the bag, retrieves
the lobster, red as a sunburn.
Shouldn't we have an epi-pen? I ask.
She points to the red ER sign,
We're right here.

In the near dark, she devours the lobster.
We walk quietly across the parking lot
into the hospital. Her face buttery
and already swelling, she smiles,
Perfect Mother's Day.

MY MOTHER AS TIGER TAMER
AT THE PSYCHIATRIC DAY CENTER

At the circus my mom organized for fun Friday,
the schizophrenics and I applaud
as she thrusts a hula hoop
with red ribbons dangling like flames
in front of Rebel, our golden retriever
whose coat she's streaked
with black paint.

With my riding crop
she points into the center
of the hula hoop and shouts, *Jump!*
Rebel springs through the hoop,
and Mom spins to face us.
In her red coat, arms outstretched, she bows.

Malaika King Albrecht

GRANDMA BEAN AND AMANI
PLAYING WITH THE DOLLHOUSE

This will be her kitchen, Amani says.
She's making sugar cookies.

Okay. I like cookies, Bean says,
but are rats good cooks?

Amani laughs. *Patty Ratty is.*
She can do anything. Even
climb stairs. Remember?

Amani drops a piece of brie
on the top stair, and Patty Ratty
races to the second floor
and eats the cheese.

Pointing, she says, *This will be*
her bedroom. We'll train her
to get into bed. Maybe
we'll teach her to go potty.

She places a bit of cheese
on the toilet rim. Patty Ratty sniffs,
scurries into the bathroom,
and snatches the cheese.

Bean holds her hand over her mouth,
hiding laughter. Tears in her eyes,
she jokes, *Your mom's not going to want*
a rat living in your dollhouse.

Maybe it can be her vacation home.

DANCING WITH MOTHER

From her metal bed in the living room,
she likes to watch the ruby throat
who guards the hummingbird feeders.
As if to impale, he darts
from the highest branch of the dogwood
straight at any intruder. She says,
The smaller the bird, the bigger the fight.

Through the screen door, I hear rain frogs
warning of a summer storm. She asks,
*Can you refill the feeders? The nectar's
in the…* She stutters, *The uh. The thing.*
The fridge? I ask. She waves me along
and stares out the window again.

Walking from the kitchen, I see
her red night gown on the floor
by the open door. Outside though the sun
shines brightly, there's a gentle rain.
Less than 90 pounds wet, she is
dancing in her underwear and bra
in the rain, and what can I do
but join her, laughing and crying.

Malaika King Albrecht

THE PACT

Amani waits by the bathtub
for the steaming hot water
to cool before she talks my mother
into folding up her long legs,
so that she can slip into the water too.

She says, *Pretend we're mermaids,*
and we've followed a ship
far away. Everyone misses us,
but we can't get back home.
My daughter splashes
her hand like a tail, and my mother's
hand follows, swimming behind her.

Wait up, Malaika. My mother says,
calling her by my name.
My daughter stops playing.
I'm Amani. Remember?
My mother apologizes. *Of course,*
Weasel. I know that.

Don't worry, Bean. If you forget,
I remember. It's like this: I'm
your granddaughter. I'm probably
your favorite. We like Patty Ratty,
your pet rat, and playing mermaids.
I can fix your hair in twists
but not braids, and you read
to me in the green chair.

My mother laughs. *Yes, and we like*
your mommy's chocolate
that she hides in a drawer.
You'll just have to remind me
which one.

THE GREAT BLUE HERON ROOKERY

Mid-March the great blue herons return
to the cypress trees above Beaver Pond.
My dad takes her hand for their daily walk,
guides her along the dirt path. My daughters
and I trail behind them. Serena taps
her *snake stick* every few steps
despite Amani's warning that she's knocking
on their dirt doors, just asking for trouble.

We enter the clearing, into this noisy place
of heavy wings, clicking beaks, and squawking,
the endless fussing over the details of life.
Quietly he counts to her, *15. 16. There are 17*
nests this year. 3 more than last year.
She says, *Yes* though she cannot remember
last year and may not even remember
yesterday's walk. I want to ask,

How can you do this everyday?
With a harsh warning croak, one bird
startles from the marshy edge.
With wings nearly a 6 foot span, the bird
flies into the open window of the sky.
Her face tilted upward, my mom says
She's beautiful. He smiles watching her,
and gray-white feathers rise in the wind
around us like ashes after a great fire.

Malaika King Albrecht

THE DAY MOM FORGETS HOW TO GET OUT OF THE CAR

Mom wrestles with the seat belt.
What's wrong with you?
she yells. *You've tied me in here.*

No, I say. *It's the seatbelt.*
I reach across her, undo the belt,
and take her hand. *Just step out.*

Her legs are stiff, she won't
swing them out of the car door.
I pull her knees towards me,

try to lift her, but she grabs
the steering wheel. She clenches
her jaw until her lips blanch.

With her free hand,
she swats at me, screams,
Stop it. Leave me here to die.

Then she cusses, such a string of words.
For a moment I'm almost glad
she remembers them.

AN ORDINARY MORNING

Sitting in her wheelchair
in her yellow nightgown,
she seems herself.
She knows my name
and that I am
her daughter.
She bites the banana
I've just given her
with the peel still on
and chews.

Malaika King Albrecht

THE LAST DANCE

Grandma Doh lifts her daughter,
my mother to her feet. She sways
unsteady until Grandma's sturdy arms
encircle her. My daughters follow
the women with their own dance
that's neither ballet nor waltz,
but an interpretive dance known to all children.

Look at me, Grandma Play-Doh.
Look at me, Bean.
My daughters vie for attention.

My mother, her wild hair white
as a cotton ball, sings loudly
and off key to my Grandma
who taught piano and voice.
Dance, dance wherever you may be.
My Grandma's agile light voice joins her,
I am the Lord of the dance, said he.

There's no safe place to look
in this room. But who can turn away?
These two women who have fought
all of my life, smile awkwardly
in each other's arms
spinning and singing on the butterfly rug.

SHE WOULD MARRY HIM AGAIN

She thinks I'm her hairdresser.
I tell her my name's Ann,
which it isn't, but it's
an easy name. I call her Patty
and bend her head over the sink
to wash her white hair
with gardenia shampoo.

When I ask if she has children,
she laughs, *I'm too young.*
I'm not even married yet.
I say, *Of course, I knew that.*
I tell her I've heard that she dates
a doctor named John
who says he wants to marry her
and grow old together.

Suddenly she sits up
soap on top of her head,
tears in her eyes.
She says, *I love him too.*
When he asks me, I'll say yes.

When I recount this story
to my father, he walks over
to her hospital bed, says,
Patty, will you marry me,
but to hell with growing old.

Malaika King Albrecht

WHAT GRANDPA WROTE TO MOM

Grandpa Dan had hands like
baseball gloves- hands that could steer
his semi in an Iowa snowstorm
and safely back home, that could land
on the shoulder of a teenage son
and restore order, that could squeeze
a young suitor nearly to his knees.

He had nicknames for everybody,
especially for her previous boyfriends,
like Barking Boy, the young man
whose voice broke when he first spoke,
Elvis for the one who dared to ask
her to a dance, and even Jo-Jo
the dog-faced boy who mom said
didn't deserve the name.

When he heard that she was engaged
to a doctor in Africa, he took
a pen in his left hand
and wrote two sentences:
I said marry a rich doctor
not a witch doctor.

THE GIFT

Serena brings a flowering branch
of the purple butterfly bush
inside to my mother. She says,
Bean, I tried to get you a pretty butterfly
just like the ones on your rug,
but they keep flying away.

Taking the twig gently in her hand,
my mother says, *One day*
I'd love a daughter just like you.
Serena stands there smiling,
looking just like me.

Malaika King Albrecht

CLEANING OUT HER CLOSET

How quickly I fill four black bags,
knot them shut for Goodwill.
I tug the silk safari scarf out one bag.
On its fabric, a Serengeti of lions,
zebras, gazelles. Dad bought it
because it resembled Tanzania
where they were married.

On the top shelf, I find her Peace Corps letters
with their stories of life in Hargeisa,
of the woman who threw a stone at her,
and how she picked it up, winged
it right back at her, how the women
laughed and became friends.

Stories of their boss Sargent Shriver
who has Alzheimer's too
and who my mom once danced with
and later wrote to a sister
He does a mean twist.
Of the small deer-like dik dik
who walked in circles until he died.

I wash the scarf in the sink,
hang it to dry in the river breeze.
Mom snores, freshly bathed
and zippered into a terry cloth gown
the color of sand, savanna grass, deer hide.

My nephew Max points at the scarf
blowing in the wind, says *Cape. Cape.*
My sister ties it still damp

around his bare shoulders.
He charges inside
with only the cape and his diaper on,
wakes Mom up, screaming *Roar!*

Malaika King Albrecht

LESSONS IN FORGETTING

Light a cigarette
    while another one
        burns in the ashtray.

Lose keys, your purse,
    credit cards, earrings,
        reading glasses, the way home.

Call your daughter your sister's name.
    Call the puppy
        the dead dog's name.

Hit the gas
    instead of the brakes.
        Slam into the van in front of you.

Turn the wrong way out of the bathroom.
    Stand in front of the wall looking for a door.
        Yell, *My bedroom is gone.*

Say you don't have
    children or a husband
        and want your daddy.

Learn to see dead family members
    in the dark. Over
        and over, call to them.

THAT WEDNESDAY AFTERNOON

Mom, help! Amani screams.
When I run into the room, she's
crying, pointing at my mother
whose right hand's wrapped
tightly around something white
that suddenly squirms, bites
my mother's index finger.

Her hand opens, and Patty Ratty
leaps onto the wooden floor, scampers
under the metal bed. My mother
confused at her bleeding finger,
starts to cry. Amani stammers
I thought she'd remember
Patty Ratty. I thought she'd
want to hold her.

Malaika King Albrecht

MY MOTHER'S FEVER

Her lips chap, then crack
and bleed. Her cheeks
blush red, her white hair
sticks to her forehead.
My oldest daughter asks,
Is she in pain?
and what can I reply
but *No. I don't think so.*

On the third morning
standing on their deck,
we watch wind gusts catch
the autumn leaves. As if
suspended by fishing line,
leaves dangle above the river
for moments before falling
into the dark water.

The sun cuts through high
grey clouds in radiant beams.
My youngest daughter who
attends a church preschool says,
Look. There are angels
sliding down those poles of light
like firefighters. Maybe
they're coming for Grandma.
As if someone can rescue her
from this burning body.

MY FATHER TEACHING MY ELDEST DAUGHTER

Fill the basin with about three inches
of warm water and add a splash of baby oil.

Begin with her eyes. With a cotton ball,
move from the inside corner of one eye

and wipe outward. Do this to both eyes,
then gently wash the rest of her face.

Make sure to clean behind her ears
where drool and spit-up collect.

He stops talking. My daughter's hands caress
my mother's forehead, which relaxes.

Mom opens her eyes and looks up at them.
Her wet face is beautiful in my daughter's hands.

Malaika King Albrecht

WE THINK SHE'S TALKING TO US

Lydia swears Mom gave her
the middle finger
in response to her question,
And how are you today?
I say she imagined it.

She wants to believe our Mom's
in there somewhere.
The only word Mom says
is *Yes*, so I ask,
Do you want more yogurt?
More chocolate? More juice?
I want to ask other questions,
but the answer's rigged.

If she yelled *Pissant* again,
we'd fight over
who she was saying it to
or about. This insult
that came to mean
endearment. A near miss,
an almost *I remember you.*

MY MOTHER'S TRANSFORMATION

This woman whose feet
have curled into bird's claws.
This woman who no longer speaks,
who sometimes whistles a note,
whose lungs knock like a woodpecker.
Whose arms bend so close,
they're wings and putting on
a nightgown is nearly impossible.

Whose mouth opens for yogurt,
for smoothies, for chocolate shakes,
and sometimes I wonder if she knows
the difference. Though today I spooned
a raspberry into her mouth,
and she drew her lips
tight as a beak, refused to eat.
This woman whose white
plume of hair grows wilder:

she will not leave this hospital bed
feathered with stuffed animals. She
will not jump. She cannot
even perch on the bed's edge. She
will not jump. She will not
fly, and no one can
push her.

Malaika King Albrecht

WHAT THEY SAID WAS COMING

The March snowstorm crushes
the early daffodils on the hill.
Nearly a foot of snow. *Don't worry*
I say as I feed her yogurt.
The snow falls on everyone.
It's nothing personal.

Her mattress, like a mad set of lungs,
inflates, deflates different sections
to ward off bed sores. The *on*
button splashes her face green.
She's not listening but opens her mouth
when the spoon touches her lips.

Suddenly the electricity goes off.
Everything holds its breath,
even the bed. Outside an owl
announces it's hungry, lonely
or both, and the low moon lights a path
across Menokin Bay
and down Cat Point Creek
to the new bridge into town.

I think someone's knocking,
but it's only that one bold deer
thumping the bird feeder with her soft nose
until it tips and spills. I feel like I did
when I brought Amani home
from the hospital. After several
nights up nursing, I was startled
to realize someone was watching me.
I stared into the stranger's eyes

only to find myself looking at myself
in the hallway mirror at 3 am.

Mother's skin's pale and thin
as tissue. She's nearly translucent
and is watching me. Her breathing's
soft and slow. For a moment
I think she could levitate or maybe I can.
I light the gas fire with a match,
and she says *Cold.* The first word
she's spoken in months. I think
*We're as prepared as anyone can be-
she and I here in the near dark.*

Malaika King Albrecht

HOW TO STAY AFLOAT

This morning, he's gone when we wake up.
Amani says, *Where's Pop Pop?*
Did he go to get biscuits?
I walk outside, and his car's there,
and in the driveway,
the empty canoe stand.
He's been threatening
to lug that old dugout canoe
into Cat Point Creek and paddle
to the small island in Menokin Bay.

On the pier I stand in the morning fog
and cold drizzle and scan the water
for movement. Nothing.
Then I hear him whistling a song.
I step to the edge of the dock
and see him. Floating with the outgoing tide
towards home, he kneels
in the canoe, bailing with a kitchen pot.
On all sides, water breaches
the canoe gunnels. He sees me
and yells, *See. She still floats.*

WHERE I FIND HER

She's in a bite of my Irish stew
and a sip of old coffee.
She's in my kitchen in her *Self-Portrait
with Phone* in a cadmium red sweater.
She hangs in my closet
in a favorite hand-me-down dress,
in the gardenia soap my sister gives me,
and in the curled *M* of my handwriting.

She's in the whippoorwill's call,
the erratic flight of the woodpecker
from the longleaf pine to the oak
and its ghostly *knock-knock-knock*.
She's in the car that peels out
in front of me, so that I catch the license plate
with her name *Patsride*.
She's the stoplight that gives me a moment
to enjoy roadside forsythia,
its yellow lack of restraint.

I find her in a brown speck in my eye,
the half moons of my nails, the slight gap
between my two front teeth.
She's everywhere, even my sleep
where she walks again. But she's not
in that body with its broken window
of a smile and its every day
incremental goodbyes.

Malaika King Albrecht

THE GROWING LIST

Serena lost a tooth.
Where's your curried chicken recipe?
Amani has her first crush.
Your poem "Earth Mother"
was published.
He had an affair.
Geneva started preschool,
and Christian turned 13.
Grandma died.
Lydia had a baby boy.
Dad's blood pressure's high.
We moved again.
Brian turned 40 years old
and won a marathon the same day.
Aunt Susan still talks
about that time you two
fooled the nun
who thought it was water
in your fishless tank.
They found a spot
on my thyroid. Sometimes I
start to dial your number
before I remember.

THE RIDDLE SONG

Grocery bags in my arms,
I hip the front door open
and hear my father singing
to my mother,
I gave my love a cherry
that had no stone.
He stretches her right leg,
then slowly rotates it in circles.

She hasn't walked in three years
or gotten out of bed in two.
I gave my love a baby
with no crying.
Her legs resist, the muscles
tight as fists. He massages
her leg nearly straight, moves
to the next one still singing.
A baby when it's sleeping
it's not crying.
The story of how I love you
it has no end.

Of course I'm crying
in the kitchen doorway.
I can't see her from here,
but I'm hoping that she's awake,
looking directly into his eyes.
He moves to her left arm,
tucked beside her body
like a broken wing,
and gently spreads it out.

Malaika King Albrecht

A RAINY SATURDAY AFTERNOON

Standing at the head of Mom's bed,
Amani and Serena blow bubbles.

Their cousin Christian points at one
the size of baby Geneva's hand,

says, *Look, Grandma. A bubble.*
It's like a round rainbow.

The bubble drifts towards the turning
ceiling fan, and Mom blinks.

Christian whispers, *I think she sees it.*
Blow more.

Serena sends a quick strand of tiny bubbles
into the air, and Amani slowly blows

a single large bubble.
Geneva grabs her brother's knees. *Up. Up.*

Christian lifts her like she's flying.
She grabs fistfuls of bubbles, laughing.

Oh, a baby, Mom says. *A baby.*

SHE'S FORGOTTEN THAT SHE
USED TO SMOKE

How often did she singe her eye brows
leaning too close to the small blue ring
of fire from the stove's gas burner,
a cigarette dangling from her lips,
drunk on boxed white wine?

Because it's June 6, we give Mom
birthday wine in a baby bottle
and a single chocolate square.
She does not ask for more.
No candles or even cake.

She sleeps, her mouth
open like she might speak.
In the dark kitchen, the pilot light
is a single blue eye,
blue as the spark that strikes
us alive and burns through
our lives like we're paper.

The same flame
that will extinguish
with her last exhalation,
a soft white moth lifting from her mouth,
wheeling upwards from this hospital bed,
drunk on light,
a wisp of smoke on her lips.

Malaika King Albrecht

HOW TO THANK HIM

I'd write a letter to Oprah
but he'd be embarrassed
and definitely wouldn't want a makeover.
I'd buy him a gift certificate
but Wal-Mart's the closest store
in Tappahannock, the next town over
and he has too much to do already.

So instead I'm writing a manual
How to Joke Your Way through Any Crisis,
and I'm dedicating it to him.
The cover will be a photo of the t-shirt
he gave me when I had kidney stones
that reads *This too shall pass.*

Everyone who reads our book
will get a lump of coal like the one
he and I have traded back and forth
for more than 20 Christmases.
Of course, I will autograph the book for him,
Dear Dad,
Thank you for taking care of my mom.
If you die, I'll kill you. Love, you know who.

MOTHER LEAVING THE FIELD
OF FORGET-ME-NOTS

She doesn't see us waving
at the edge of the field,
our arms mere wheat in the wind.
She holds no love or grudges.

The past shrinks, an indistinct
point on the horizon. All's forgiven.
She's flying her hat, running through
the pure blue toward what might be light.

Malaika King Albrecht

ERASURE

I. of The Pact

Amani waits by the bathtub
for the steaming hot water
to cool before she talks **my mother**
into folding up her long legs,
so that she can slip in the water too.

She says, *Pretend we're mermaids,*
and we've followed a ship
far away. Everyone misses us,
but we **can't get back** *home.*
My daughter splashes
her hand like a tail, and my mother's
hand follows, swimming behind her.

Wait up, Malaika. My mother says,
calling my daughter by my name.
My daughter stops playing.
I'm Amani **Remember?**
My mother apologizes. *Of course,*
Weasel. I know that.

Don't worry, Bean. If you forget,
I remember. It's like this: I'm your
granddaughter. I'm probably
your favorite. We like Patty Ratty,
your pet rat, and playing mermaids.
I can fix your hair in twists
but not braids and you read
to me in the green chair.

My mother laughs. *Yes, and we like*
your mommy's chocolate
that she **hides in a drawer**.
You'll just have to remind me
which one.

II. of The Great Blue Heron Rookery

Mid-March the great blue herons return
To the cypress trees above Beaver Pond.
My dad **takes Mom's hand** for their daily walk,
guides her along the dirt path. My daughters
and I trail behind them. Serena taps
her *snake stick* every few steps
despite Amani's warning that she's knocking
on their dirt doors, just asking for trouble.

We enter the clearing, into this noisy place
of heavy wings, clicking beaks, and squawking,
the endless fussing over the details of life.
Quietly he counts to her, *15. 16. There are 17*
nests this year. 3 more than last year.
She says, *Yes* though she cannot **remember**
last year and may not even remember
yesterday's walk. I want to ask,

How can you do this every day?
With a harsh warning croak, one heron
startles from the marshy edge.
With wings nearly a 6 foot span, the heron
flies into **the open window of** the sky.
Her face tilted upward, my mom says,
She's beautiful. He **smile**s watching her,
and gray-white feathers rise in the wind
around us like ashes after a great fire.

III. of She Would Marry Him Again

She thinks I'm her hairdresser.
I tell her my name's Ann,
which it isn't, but it's
an easy name. I call her Patty
and bend her head over the sink
to wash her white hair
with gardenia shampoo.

When I ask if she has children,
she laughs, *I'm too young.*
I'm not even married yet.
I say, *Of course, I knew that.*
I tell her I've heard that she dates
a doctor named John
who **says** he wants to marry her
and grow old together.
Suddenly she sits up
soap on top of her head,
tears in her eyes.
she says, *I love him too.*
When he asks me, I'll say **yes**.

When I recount this story
to my father, he walks over
to her hospital bed, says,
Patty, will you marry me,
but to hell with growing old.

IV. of My Mother's Fever

Her lips chap, then crack
and bleed. Her cheeks
blush red, her white hair
sticks to her forehead.
My oldest daughter asks,
Is she *in pain?*
and what can I reply
but *No. I don't think so.*

On the third morning
standing on their deck,
we watch wind gusts catch
the autumn leaves. As if
suspended by fishing line,
leaves dangle **above** the river
for moments before falling
into the dark water.

The sun cuts through high
grey clouds in radiant beams.
My youngest daughter who
attends a church preschool says,
Look. There are angels
sliding down those poles of light
like firefighters. Maybe
they're coming for Grandma.
As if someone can rescue **her**
from this **burning** body.

Malaika King Albrecht

V. of What They Said was Coming

The March snowstorm crushes
the early daffodils on the hill.
Nearly a foot of snow. *Don't worry*
I say as I feed her yogurt.
The snow falls *on everyone.*
It's nothing personal.

Her mattress, like a mad set of lungs,
inflates, deflates different sections
to ward off bed sores. The *on*
button splashes her face green.
She's not listening but **opens her mouth**
when the spoon touches her lips.

Suddenly the electricity goes off.
Everything holds its **breath,**
even the bed. Outside an owl
announces it's hungry, lonely
or both, and the low moon lights a path
across Menokin Bay
and down Cat Point Creek
to **the** new **bridge** into town.

I think someone's knocking,
but it's only that one bold deer
thumping the bird feeder with her soft nose
until it tips and spills. I feel like I did
when I brought Amani home
from the hospital. After several
nights up nursing, **I** was startled
to **realize** someone was watching me.
I stared into the stranger's eyes

only to find myself looking at myself
in the hallway mirror at 3 am.

Mother's skin's pale and thin
as tissue. **She's nearly** translucent
and is watching me. Her breathing's
soft and slow. For a moment
I think she could levitate or maybe I can.
I light the gas fire with a match,
and she says *Cold*. The first word
she's spoken in months. I think
*We're as **prepared** as anyone can be-
she and I here in **the** near **dark.***

VI. of The Riddle Song

Grocery bags in my arms,
I hip the front door open
and hear my father singing
to my mother,
*I gave **my love** a cherry
that had no stone.*
He stretches her right leg,
then slowly rotates it in circles.

She hasn't walked in three years
or gotten out of bed in two.
*I gave my love **a** baby
with no crying.*
Her legs resist, the muscles
tight as fists. He massages
her leg nearly straight, moves
to the next one still singing.
A baby when it's sleeping

Malaika King Albrecht

it's not crying.
The story of how I love you
it has no end.

Of course I'm crying
in the kitchen doorway.
I can't see her from here,
but I'm hoping that she's awake,
looking directly into his eyes.
He moves to her left arm,
tucked beside her body
like a broken **wing**
and gently spreads it out.

VII. of Mother Leaving the Field of Forget Me Nots

She doesn't see us waving
at the edge of the field,
our arms mere wheat in the wind.
She holds no love or grudges.

The past shrinks, an indistinct
point on the horizon. All**'s** forgiven.
She's flying her hat, running through
the pure blue toward what might be **light.**